Dedication

I dedicate this book to my son Cody who is my best treasure in life. I am also grateful to my fossil friends, John Walker, Glen Kuban, Brian Johnson and Dona Hanks. They have shared my excitement, pulled me out of mud holes, helped carry my heavy buckets and are true friends.

Forward

I hope you enjoy this treasure hunting guide. I have been treasure hunting for many years and love the thrill of the adventure! Finding old historical items, extinct animal bones and cool rocks is really exciting. There are many wonderful places in the U.S. to hunt for treasure of all kinds. You might even be able to make money from the treasures you find. Remember to respect the earth, clean up your litter and appreciate each treasure find you get.

TABLE OF CONTENTS

- Note for Parents   3
- Safety and Precautions   4
- Supplies you need   5
- Different kinds of treasure   6
- How to find treasure   7
- Metal detecting   8
- Fossils and bones   9
- Gemstones and Cool rocks   10
- Artifacts   10
- Coins, Stamps and Collectibles   11
- Treasure Hunting Places   12
- My Favorite Places for treasure   14
- Keep Records and Labels   33
- Treasure Hunting Log Sheet   34
- Order Dinosaur tracks   35
- Links to state by state listing of fossil   35
  and rock sites

NOTE FOR PARENTS

Treasure hunting is great fun for kids and the whole family! Kids love all kinds of treasure and this book will help them get started.

Here are just some of the reasons to get your kids involved with treasure hunting:

- It gets them off the couch, away from video games and computers and outside in the fresh air.

- This is great for exercise, getting muddy sometimes and having fun.

- It allows your children to be interesting in learning about the history of a location and the age of an old artifact.

- Treasure hunting helps them learn to take care of the earth, history and artifacts of the earth.

- It is affordable, family fun! There are tons of FREE places to look for treasure. Many of the pay sites for treasure hunting are easily affordable. You can have great bonding time as a family.

SAFETY AND PRECAUTIONS

Sharp edges – many fossil shark teeth, gemstones and some artifacts have very sharp edges. Be careful of the age of the child versus the danger of the object they find.

Tools – make sure young children only use a plastic shovel without the pointed sharp tip. Older children can use metal shovels. Be careful of hammers, chisels, shovels and other tools around kids. Help them use the tools safely and supervise them at all times.

Sanitation – Wash your hands after playing in the dirt or water. Take portable hand sanitizer wipes with you. I use baby wipes in my bucket. Make sure you have permission for the location you are hunting. Don't randomly walk on someone's land and start looking. Ask first!

SUPPLIES YOU NEED

I use a small bucket with a handle and I put my tools in that. That way I have everything I need in my one bucket.

- Plastic sandwich bags and grocery bags to put your finds in. Also newspaper to wrap fragile items.

- A few bottles of water – at least one in your bucket at all times. Don't forget snacks or lunch.

- Small plastic shovel, small trowel, small hammer, and screwdriver

- Insect repellant and hand sanitizer wipes

- Extra T-shirt, bandana or a few rags

- Whistle for safety, garden gloves

- Sometimes cheap rubber boots (if muddy or going in water)

DIFFERENT KINDS OF TREASURE

Fossils, dinosaur tracks and bones

shark teeth

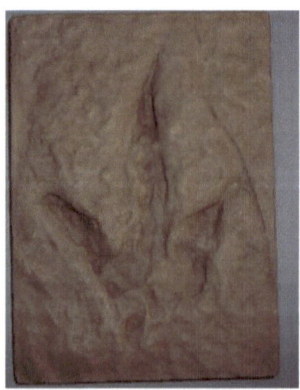

dinosaur track

whale vertebrae

Gemstones, cool rocks, arrowheads

smoky quartz

amethyst

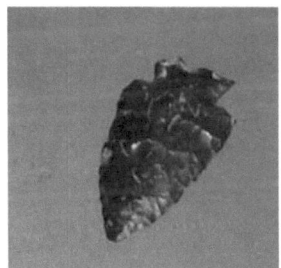
indian arrowhead

Metal detecting for artifacts

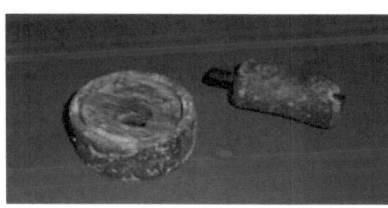
old ship parts

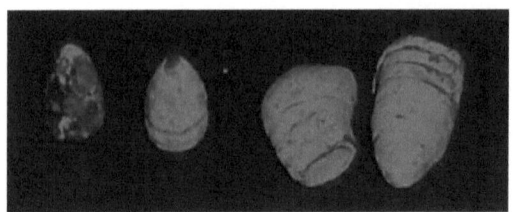

civil war bullets

HOW TO FIND TREASURE

Start by checking the history of your own town. How old is the town and was the Revolutionary or Civil wars fought there? Was it old Indian territory? Check your library for local historical maps for what used to be on the land. I usually check where the old garbage dump was, dried up riverbeds and any historical sites in the area.

Once you have the information about your own town, you'll be able to narrow down where to start looking. Keep in mind that people used to bury their garbage in their yards before modern trash service and landfills. Old outhouse buildings are a great place to look for old treasure.

Metal Detecting

A metal detector is a great way to find treasure! It picks up on coins, jewelry and most types of metal. You can ask your parents for a youth metal detector or save your allowance and get your own! They range in price from $ 35 to $1,000. I have found lots of stuff with my $200 metal detector.

If you have a metal detector, start with your own backyard. Dig small holes where the metal detector beeps and cover the holes when you are done. You can also metal detect in local parks, swimming holes or beaches. Older properties are a great place to metal detect, battlefields or old military campsites. Remember to get permission and check rules before metal detecting.

Fossils and bones

Most fossils are near the beaches and on islands near the beaches. Fossils can also be found where they cut mountains to make roads (road cuts). There are also big rock quarries and special sites where you can hunt for old fossils.

Gemstones, Gold and Cool Rocks

Mostly you will find gems and cool rocks around streams and riverbeds. Most gold panning is done in the streams. There are lots of gem mining sites in NC where you can pay to sift through buckets of gems. This is tons of fun for the whole family! The also have specific emerald and ruby mines to hunt for treasure.

Artifacts

Old artifacts are everywhere! If you are looking for arrowheads and Indian rocks, check your local farm fields. Ask a local farmer if you can check his field after he turns the soil. That's the best time. Another good spot is near riverbanks and streams.

I also like to hunt for old coins, old civil war buttons, buckles and old pottery. Some have been found with the metal detector and some just by digging around old campsites, old property, beaches and riverbanks. I also have a collection of old bottles with thick glass in different colors. You can ask someone with an old house or property if you can metal detect around the yard or barn. Then split the profit of what you find or split the treasure.

Old bottles

Collectibles

You can start saving coins, stamps, comic books or old toys. Pick something you would like to collect and check flea markets, garage sales to add to your collection a little bit at a time. When you are older they could be worth a money.

LIST OF TREASURE HUNTING PLACES

The Eastern Coast Shoreline

The eastern coast shoreline is full of fossils around the beaches and further inland. Remember that much of what is land now was once ocean water.

The eastern coast is also the beginning point of many immigrants who came to this country. The history of people, houses, towns and cool artifacts dates around 1650-1900. The first places that were settled and the oldest towns are Charleston, SC, Savannah, GA, Virginia and New England .

Great places to look for artifacts would be old farms, old houses and properties, old swimming holes and parks, dry riverbeds. Some great fossil hot spots along the coast are Florida, Georgia, South Carolina, North Carolina, Virginia and Maryland.

The Southeast

Arkansas has diamonds and Diamond Head State Park is free to the public and you can search the dirt fields for diamonds. Many people have found valuable diamonds there. Alabama, Georgia, South Carolina and Mississippi also have great fossils, rocks and artifacts.

The Middle Section of US

Illinois, Indiana and Kansas have great fossils. Many states in the middle section of the country have great fossils and rocks.

Western Section of US

I lived in Colorado for five years and have had tons of fun finding artifacts, fossils and rocks in the Wild West.

There are big fish quarries in Wyoming. There are numerous dinosaur digs in Montana and Wyoming that kids and adults can do. There are cool rocks, fossils and dinosaur tracks in Utah. There is also a geode place you can hunt near

Toole, Utah. Gold panning is a big part of treasure hunting in Colorado, California, Nevada and other western states.   There are also old mining towns to find artifacts.   In the lower section of Colorado you can find plant, leaf and insect fossils. They are in pieces of shale rock that you split open.

Be sure and see the complete state by state list of fossils and rocks on the resource page in the back of the book.

My Favorite Places

NC - Spruce Pine / Burnsville

The Gem Mine in NC is easy. Just buy a bucket, put it through a water trowel and get awesome gemstones! I've done this mine about fifty times and am never disappointed. Some of the gems are in "rough" form, like some of the garnet and sapphires.   Pay attention to what the rough form looks like.

Citrine

Garnet / Emerald

Charleston, SC

I lived in Charleston, SC for a few years and was grateful to have a small boat to explore the rivers. The history in Charleston is very old and includes Fort Sumter, where the Civil War began. The Revolutionary War was also fought there. There were even once pirates there with many of their own treasure stories. On some of the islands I discovered they were old war campsites for the soldiers. I found lots of cool pottery, bullets from the civil war and revolutionary war. There were even bullets sticking out of some of the trees on the island. My favorite artifact is a trigger handle from a Revolutionary War musket (gun).

Trigger guard from Revolutionary Gun

1671 old pottery

old colonial pottery

old Indian pottery

I also found many shark teeth, disks, whale bones, extinct seashells on some of the islands around Charleston.

inner ear bones –whale

extinct sea shells

shark spine disks

One of my best Charleston finds was a fossil turtle skull. It took a few months for my friend and I to dig it out of a tidal creek. We had no clue what it was, but we knew it was something fossil related. I had to send it to a professional fossil lab for cleaning and then it went to the

Black Hills Institute in South Dakota for identification. It turns out to be a pretty rare turtle skull, with the species named Carolinachelys wilsoni. It is approximately 25 million years old and I named him Ralph.

Hilton Head, SC

The beaches and islands of Hilton Head are one of my favorite spots for fossil hunting and artifacts. The fossils from this area are about 25 million years old. I've found many shark teeth (some big ones), lots of shark disks, whale bones, turtle pieces and even a wooly mammoth tooth!

wooly mammoth back tooth

Sting ray mouth plates

various shark teeth

Whale vertebrae

In Hilton Head I go out on a boat with my fossil friend. We hunt the outer islands around Hilton Head. We have had many fossil adventures together and have found some really cool stuff.

Some of these islands are called "dredged" islands. This means they pump up sand and dirt from the bottom of rivers through big pipes and dump them on islands. Some of the islands are actually created from dredging the rivers and dumping on the islands. The reason they dredge the rivers is to made them deeper and wider for big barges, boats and even cruise ships to get through.

I also search the beaches with my metal detector for tourist treasure. Also in Charleston and Hilton Head, old shipwreck stuff washes up on the beach sometimes, like pottery and ship parts.

Green River, Wyoming

One of the most beautiful places in the country and full of fish fossils, sometimes rare stingrays and shrimp fossils. There are several big fish quarries around Green River and Kemmerer Wyoming. I went to one quarry with a fossil friend of mine and it was some of the hardest work we've ever done. Big sheets of heavy shale that we split open to find cool fish. These fish are around 150 million years old.

prehistoric fish fossils

Delta, Utah

Delta, Utah is also a beautiful place, desolate and really cool. There is a quarry where you can dig for trilobites and split shale. Trilobites are one of the first sea creatures. It looks like a swimming bug. Trilobites are 450 million years old. You pay a small fee, they give you some tools and instructions and you can go dig in the quarry. You can take home what you find. There are lots of different species of trilobites so they are all different.

trilobites

Undisclosed, Utah

In the middle of a desert near some old railroad tracks is a surprising pile of the most beautiful rock you've ever seen. It is called Wonderstone and has spirals and patterns of different colors and designs. The designs are made from when lava once flowed over the rock which form the cool patterns and colors. I got lots of this cool rock on one of my trips and polished some, made jewelry out of others. It is very different from any other rocks I've found. You can find

Wonderstone around Utah, Nevada and parts of California.

 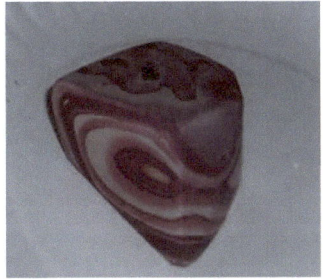

wonderstone

Old Gold Mine in Boulder, CO

This old gold mine also has an old refinery where they processed the gold after mining it. There was once a whole town here and much of the equipment remains. I've found a bobcat inner ear bone fossil, several old bottles, a cool metal top from an old lantern. My favorite is a piece of metal / pottery from the top of an old woodstove from the 1800's.

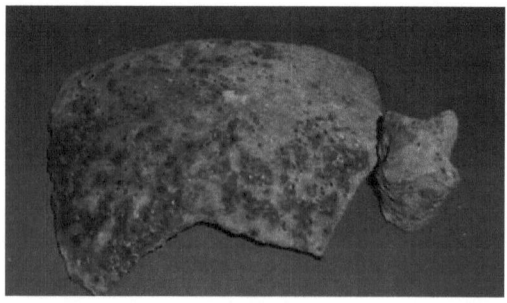

Nevadaville, CO

This is a cool town in Colorado that once had 40,000 people. Now there are six people living there. They ran out of water. There are still old gold mines and a few active gold mines in the area, but the town is gone. I searched around the hillsides where the old houses used to be because I could still see the partial stone wallsof the old houses.   I found this collection of old pottery and old glass.

old pottery/glass

abandoned house

City hall abandoned

Florrisant, CO

There is a little quarry here with shale that is easy to split. Leaves, plants and cool insects can be found in the shale. It is approximately 35 million years old. There is a little picnic table where you can sit in the shade and split the shale from the piles. I have found numerous plant fossils, a few spiders and a cool fossil bee while treasure hunting there. Many of these fossils go to museums around the country. If you have extra time, close by the quarry is a large Petrified Wood site you can tour.

leaf fossil

Southern Colorado – Rocks and Fossils

While exploring the National Forest around Lake George, CO a friend and I discovered lots of smoky quartz and amazonite gems. He had a friend with a mining claim in the area and we also got to hunt his friend's land. His friend uses big bulldozers to dig in the land to pull out huge pieces of smoky quartz and amazonite. We just looked around the dirt on the surface. Here's just some of what we found out there in a days time.

Amazonite (above)

Smoky Quartz & points

Northern Nevada

This was a long, dusty trip to the Northwest tip
of Nevada on the Oregon border. This was an
opal mine and I was determined to try it once. I
was especially interested in the fire opal because
of its value.

I had no idea how far out in the wilderness this
place would be. It was a hundred miles to the
closest town and I was so grateful for the tiny
motel and restaurant close by the mine. There
are also campgrounds in the area with several
different opal mines.

My car will never forget the dust from the
desert. There were also beautiful mountains, wild
burros and giant jackrabbits. I've never driven
for so long without seeing a single house or
person.

After three days of driving, I got to the outdoor
mine which was really a giant dirt wall with large
piles of dirt all around. I followed the
instructions, watched others and dug the holes as
best as I could. I also searched the piles. I was

amazed to see the couple next to me dig out at least $25,000 worth of fire opal in two days. They were thrilled to find out what it was worth. I simply did not have enough muscle power to dig deep enough holes. I decided to search the piles.

I ended up digging out some nice black opal, several pieces of white, orange/red and some yellow opal. My favorite piece was the tiny petrified wood piece filled with fire opal. It shines with all the colors of the rainbow. Red, blue, green and yellow and is truly beautiful when held up to the sunlight. I also found a cool fossilized pine cone. If I go back again I will take a friend with muscles and a bigger shovel!

fire opal   black opal & colored

KEEP RECORDS

It is really important to label your treasure finds with certain information. The table below will help you keep track of the dates, location, items you find and perhaps the value of the item.

A proper label is like this :

Item found
Location
Age of item

Example:

Mako Shark Tooth
Hilton Head Island, SC
Approx. 25 Millions Years Old

When you are storing your treasures keep a label with them. For instance, if you keep them in plastic baggies then put a label in the baggie to identify each group of stuff. If you display your treasures on a shelf then put a little label with each one so you know where they came from.

TREASURE HUNTING LOG SHEET

Date	Location	Item Found	Age	Val

RESOURCES AND LINKS FOR MORE TREASURE HUNTING INFORMATION

Order Dinosaur tracks & fossils

You can order your own cool plaster dinosaur tracks and other fossils on my friend Glen Kuban's Website. See all his dinosaur track pictures.

http://wwww.paleo.cc/paleoscene.htm

http://paleo.cc/kpaleo.htm

For a list of fossil sites by state go to this link

http://members.fortunecity.com/michaelp2/fossil1.html

Rock Collecting Sites List by State

http://www.42explore.com/rocks2.htm

http:// www. gemandmineral.com/states.html

www.ingramcontent.com/pod-product-compliance
Lightning Source LLC
Chambersburg PA
CBHW050905290526
45792CB00002B/709